at when com

beat —

made or mended, —

rooms distended .

ning next year,

& Fanny near,

delight us

over right us. —

I. A. —

'…the remembrance of it often becomes a pleasure.'
– *Persuasion*

Frances Lincoln Limited
www.franceslincoln.com

Jane Austen Daybook
Published in association with The British Library, London
Copyright © Frances Lincoln Limited 2015
Colour illustrations and text copyright © the British Library 2015

James Edward Austen-Leigh's silhouettes and 'Chawton Cottage'
© A Room of One's Own Press.

ISBN: 978-0-7112-3632-5
Printed in China
First Frances Lincoln edition 2015
9 8 7 6 5 4 3 2 1

Front cover: Bridal dress taken from *The Repository of Arts, Literature, Commerce,
Manufactures, Fashions and Politics*, London, 1823-28. [C.119.f.1, plate 33]
Above: First quadrille at Almack's from *The Reminiscences and recollections of Captain
Gronow 1810-60*. With illustrations, from contemporary sources,
by J. Grego. London, 1889. [2406.h.1 volume 1, opposite 32]

Jane Austen

DAYBOOK

Edited by

Freydis Jane Welland

THE BRITISH LIBRARY

FRANCES LINCOLN LIMITED

PUBLISHERS

Jane Austen (1775–1817)

Jane Austen was born on 16 December 1775 to Revd. George Austen and Cassandra Leigh in the village of Steventon in the Hampshire countryside. It was at Steventon that the foundations of Jane Austen's later fame were laid. There, in 1796, at the age of 21 she began to write a novel, finishing the draft in just ten months. It was to be *Pride and Prejudice*, later completed at Chawton Cottage. The poem to her brother Frank, part of which is shown in her own handwriting on the inside covers of this Jane Austen daybook, anticipates the happiness and creativity of life at Chawton Cottage. It was at Chawton that Jane Austen wrote her mature novels, *Mansfield Park*, *First Impressions*, *Emma* and *Persuasion*.

Chawton Cottage was sometimes the scene of a family party with lively readings of Jane Austen's latest book. Her brother Henry said Jane Austen read aloud with very great taste and effect, as her voice was extremely sweet and both nature and art joined to make her a delightful reader. Her nephew James Edward Austen-Leigh, who commissioned the portrait above for his *Memoir*, described the literary life at Chawton Cottage:

In that well-occupied female party, there must have been many precious hours of silence during which the pen was busy at the little mahogany desk while Fanny Price, or Emma Woodhouse, or Anne Elliot was growing into beauty and interest.

Jane Austen wrote to her sister Cassandra on 24 October 1798 from The Bull and George at Dartford:

After we had been here a quarter of an hour, it was discovered that my writing and dressing boxes had by accident been put into a chaise which was just packing off as we came in, and were driven away towards Gravesend on their way to the West Indies. No part of my property could have been such a prize before, for in my writing-box was all my worldly wealth, 7 £.... Mr. Nottley immediately despatched a man and horse after the chaise, and in half an hour's time I had the pleasure of being as rich as ever; they were got about two or three miles off.

Jane Austen's writing desk is now on display in the Treasures Gallery of the British Library, courtesy of Joan Austen-Leigh and her daughters. It has a sloped leather top and is nicely fitted with a long drawer, a place for an inkwell, penknife and quills, and space for correspondence, spectacles and string, manuscripts, and sealing wax. The desk has had some of Jane Austen's letters and family things stored in it for generations, including the hand-tooled leather album of James Edward Austen-Leigh's silhouettes, which illustrate the pages that follow.

Jane Austen's delight was to write about three or four families in a country village. The enduring truth of her observations and the aptness of her descriptions are amply illustrated in this Jane Austen Daybook.

In July 1809 Jane Austen, together with her mother Mrs Austen, her sister Cassandra and their friend Martha Lloyd, began living in Chawton Cottage. This sparked a time of great creativity in Jane Austen's life: she wrote Mansfield Park, Emma and Persuasion there, and revised Pride and Prejudice and Sense and Sensibility. This watercolour of Chawton Cottage is believed to be by Jane Austen's niece, one of James Edward Austen-Leigh's sisters, Anna Austen, later Mrs Ben Lefroy.

'I am sorry to tell you that I am getting very extravagant & spending all my Money; & what is worse for you, I have been spending yours too... I was tempted by a pretty coloured muslin and bought 10 yards of it, on the chance of your liking it.'

– *Letter to Cassandra Austen*
18 April 1811, Sloane Street, London.

Messrs. Harding, Howell, and Co. at 89, Pall Mall, London.
Originally published in Ackermann, 1809
[Maps.K.Top.27.20, plate 12]

January

1

2

3

4

5

6

7

8

'...performances which have only genius,
wit and taste to recommend them.'

– *Northanger Abbey*

January

9

1773 Jane Austen's sister Cassandra Elizabeth Austen is born

10

11

12

THEY TALKED OF WILLIAM...

—

'With spirits, courage and curiosity up
to anything, William expressed an inclination
to hunt; and Crawford could mount him without
the slightest inconvenience to himself. [Fanny]
feared for William; by no means convinced by all
that he could relate of his own horsemanship...
nor till he returned safe and well ... could she
feel any of that obligation to Mr. Crawford
for lending the horse which he had fully
intended it should produce.'

– *Mansfield Park*, Volume II, Chapter 6

January

13

14

15   1796 Jane Austen writes to Cassandra 'I am to flirt my last with Tom Lefroy.'

16

17

18

19

20

'We acted with the best of intentions.'

– *Pride and Prejudice*

January

21

1805 Jane Austen's father, Revd. George Austen, dies
1814 Jane Austen begins *Emma*

22

23

1793 Jane Austen's niece Fanny Knight is born

24

Interior of a house from *Fragments on the Theory and Practice of Landscape Gardening* by Humphry Repton, 1816. [59.e.20, opposite 58]

January

25

26

27

1817 Jane Austen begins *Sanditon*

28

1813 *Pride and Prejudice* is published

29

30

31

'She felt truly for them all.'

– *Mansfield Park*

'William, her brother, the so long absent and dearly beloved brother was in England again. She had a letter from him herself, a few hurried happy lines, written as the ship came up Channel, and sent into Portsmouth with the first boat that left the Antwerp at anchor in Spithead.'

– *Mansfield Park*

The Royal Dock Yard at Portsmouth from *View of the Royal Dock Yard at Portsmouth*, by R. Dodd, 1790 [Maps.K.Top.14.46.a]

February

1

2

3

4

A View at CHELSEA 1784.

February

5

6

7

8

9

10

11

12

'The chance proved a lucky one...'

– Sense and Sensibility

February

13

14

15

1765 Jane Austen's oldest brother James Austen is born

16

ANNE WAS LOOKING
REMARKABLY WELL...

—

'When they came into the steps, leading
upwards from the beach, a gentleman at the
same moment preparing to come down, politely
drew back, and stopped to give them way.
They ascended and passed him; and as
they passed, Anne's face caught his eye, and
he looked at her with a degree of earnest
admiration, which she could not be insensible
of... It was evident that the gentleman
(completely a gentleman in manner) admired
her exceedingly. Captain Wentworth
looked round at her instantly...'

– Persuasion

February

17

18

19

20

21

22

23

24

'...this delightful habit of journalizing...'

– *Northanger Abbey*

February

25

26

27

28

29

'Harriet, tempted by everything
and swayed by half a word, was
always very long at a purchase...
Emma went to the door for
amusement... A mind lively
and at ease, can do with seeing
nothing, and can see nothing
that does not answer...'

– *Emma*

High Street, Putney, Surrey from *The volumes for
Berkshire, Buckinghamshire, Surrey, Essex and Hertfordshire
are lithographed,* by William Berry, London, 1837.
[Crach.1.Tab.1.b.1, before 291]

March

1

2

3

4

5

6

7

8

'Imagination is everything.'

– Letter to Cassandra, 17 November 1798, Steventon

March

9

10

11

12

...A PLEASANT RESPITE...

—

'Upon the whole it was an excellent journey
& very thoroughly enjoyed...'

– Letter to Cassandra,
20 May 1813, Sloane Street, London

March

13

14

15

16

17

18

19

20

'Let other pens dwell on guilt and misery.'

– *Mansfield Park*

March

21

22

23

24

Great Poulteney Street, Bath, seen through the gateway of Sydney Place. Jane Austen lived at 4, Sydney Place from 1801 until 1804. From a series of engravings by J. C. Nattes, 1806. [199.i.7, Plate 56]

March

25

26

27

28

March

1815 Jane Austen completes *Emma*

29

30

31

'Friendship is certainly the finest balm
for the pangs of disappointed love.'

– *Northanger Abbey*

'The Sea air & Sea Bathing together were nearly infallible... They were healing, softing, relaxing – fortifying & bracing – seemingly just as was wanted – sometimes one, sometimes the other.'

– *Sanditon*

April

1

2

3

4

THEY WENT TO THE SANDS,
TO WATCH THE FLOWING
OF THE TIDE...

—

'They praised the morning; gloried
in the sea; sympathized in the
delight of the fresh-feeling breeze —
and were silent...'

– Persuasion

April

5

6

7

8

'How quick come the reasons for approving what we like!'

– *Persuasion*

April

13

14

15

1793 Jane Austen's niece Anna Austen Lefroy is born

16

Palais-Royal, 1803, taken from *Fashion in Paris* by Octave Uzanne with illustrations by F. Courboin, London, 1898. [7742.de.8, plate 21]

April

17

18

19

20

21

22

1774 Jane Austen's brother Francis Austen is born

23

24

'I dearly love a laugh.'

– *Pride and Prejudice*

April

25 1811 Jane Austen writes to Cassandra, 'No indeed, I am never too busy to think of S&S. I can no more forget it, than a mother can forget her suckling child.'

26 1764 Revd. George Austen and Cassandra Leigh marry at Bath

27

28

Messrs. Pellatt and Green's, St. Paul's Church Yard, London. Originally published in *Ackermann*, 1809. [Maps.K.Top.27.23, plate 22]

April

29

30

'Elizabeth, as they drove along,
watched for the first appearance
of Pemberley Woods with some
perturbation; and when at length
they turned in at the lodge, her
spirits were in a high flutter.'

– *Pride and Prejudice*

A country house from *County Genealogies, etc The volumes
for Berkshire, Buckinghamshire, Surrey, Essex and Hertfordshire
are lithographed* by William Berry, 1837.
[Crach.1.Tab.1.b.1 volume 19]

May

1

2

3

4

5

6

7

8

'You must be the best judge of your own happiness.'

– Emma

May

9

1814 *Mansfield Park* published

10

11

12

NOTHING BUT PLEASURE
THE WHOLE DAY THROUGH.

—

'He lived to exert, and frequently
to enjoy himself... In his breed of horses
and dogs, and in sporting of every kind,
he found no inconsiderable degree
of domestic felicity.'

– Sense and Sensibility

May

13

14

15

16

1799 Jane Austen and her family move to Bath

'Such a trifle is not worth half so many words.'

– *Mansfield Park*

May

21

22

23

24

Winchelsea Friary and Chapel from *Grimm's Sussex Drawings*, by Samuel Hieronymus Grimm, 1784.
[Add. 5670, f.21]

May

25

26

27

28

29

30

31

'Till this moment I never knew myself'

– Pride and Prejudice

'I remember the time when I liked a red coat myself very well — and indeed so I do still at my heart; and if a smart young colonel, with five or six thousand a year, should want one of my girls, I shall not say nay to him; and I thought Colonel Forster looked very becoming the other night at Sir William's in his regimentals.'

— Pride and Prejudice

The Royal Review in Hatfield Park of the Volunteer Cavalry and Infantry, with the Militia of the County of Herts, on the 13 June 1800, by R. Livesay; engraved by Stadler, 1802 [Maps.K.Top. 15.65.e]

June

1

2

3

4

5

6

7

1771 Jane Austen's brother Henry Austen is born

8

'...her spirits danced within her...'

– *Northanger Abbey*

June

9

10

11

12

June

1790 Jane Austen finishes *Love and Freindship*

13

14

15

16

17

1805 Jane Austen's niece Caroline Austen is born

18

19

20

'...with gratitude and pleasure...'

– *Pride and Prejudice*

June

21

22

1779 Jane Austen's younger brother Charles Austen is born

23

24

...THOUGHTS OF A LITTLE
COUNTRY AIR AND QUIET!

—

'Her passion for ancient edifices was next to
her passion for Henry Tilney, and castles and
abbies made usually the charm of those reveries
which his image did not fill. To see and explore
either the ramparts and keep of one, or the
cloisters of the other, had been for many
weeks a darling wish...'

– Northanger Abbey, Volume II, Chapter 2

June

25

26

27

28

'There was consciousness, animation and warmth... '

— *Emma*

As for ourselves, we're very well;
As unaffected prose will tell,
Cassandra's pen will paint our state
The many comforts that await
Our Chawton home, how much we find
Already in it, to our mind;
And how convinced, that when complete
It will all other Houses beat
That ever have been made or mended,
With rooms concise, or rooms distended.
You'll find us very snug next year;
Perhaps with Charles and Fanny near,
For now it often does delight us
To fancy them just over-right us.

– *Poem for Francis Austen,*
26 July 1809, Chawton

July

1

2

1806 Mrs George Austen and her daughters leave Bath

3

4

5

1813 Jane Austen writes Frank, 'I have now written myself
into £250 – which only makes me long for more.'

6

1809 Mrs George Austen and her daughters move to Chawton

7

8

'She plays and sings all day long.'

– Pride and Prejudice

July

9

10

11

12

Sir Richard Arkwright's mansion, near Matlock Bath, Derbyshire. Taken from *Perspective View of Sir Richard Arkwright's House at Cromford designed by Wm. Thomas 1789 & 790 by* W. Thomas and T. Cartwright, 1805.
[Maps.2070.(1)]

July

13

14

15

16

17

1817 Jane Austen dies in Winchester, at No. 8 College Street

18

19

20

'What wild imaginations one forms where
dear self is concerned.'

– *Persuasion*

July

21

22

23

24

IT WAS A PLEASANT
FERTILE SPOT, WELL WOODED,
AND RICH IN PASTURE.

—

'As a house, Barton Cottage, though small,
was comfortable and compact; but as a cottage
it was defective, for the building was regular,
the roof was tiled, the window shutters were
not painted green, nor were the walls
covered with honeysuckles.'

– Sense and Sensibility

July

25

26

27

28

29

30

31

'They read, they talked, they sang together...'

– Sense and Sensibility

'The Orange Wine will want our Care soon.— But in the meantime for Elegance & Ease & Luxury... I shall eat Ice and drink French wine, & be above vulgar Economy. Luckily the pleasures of Friendship, of unreserved Conversation, of similarity of Taste & Opinions, will make good amends for Orange Wine.'

– Letter to Cassandra, Godmersham, Thursday, 30 June 1808

August

1

2

3

4

5

1816 Jane Austen completes *Persuasion*

6

7

1815 Jane Austen begins *Persuasion*

8

'All was joy and kindness.'

– *Pride and Prejudice*

August

9

10

11

12

Newton Bridge, near Bath. Taken from *A coloured view of Newton Bridge, near Bath.* [Maps.K.Top.38.28]

August

13

14

15

16

17

18

19

20

'If any one faculty of our nature may be called more
wonderful than the rest, I do think it is memory.'

– *Mansfield Park*

August

21

22

23

24

MR. DARCY MEETS ELIZABETH
AND THE GARDINERS BESIDE
A STREAM AT PEMBERLEY.

—

'The conversation soon turned upon fishing
and Elizabeth heard Mr. Darcy invite him,
with the greatest civility, to fish there as often
as he chose, while he continued in the
neighbourhood, offering at the same time
to supply him with fishing tackle, and
pointing out those parts of the stream
where there was usually most sport.'

– Pride and Prejudice, Volume III, Chapter 1

August

25

26

1766 Jane Austen's brother George Austen the younger is born

27

28

29

30

31

'Follies and nonsense, whims and inconsistencies do divert me,
I own, and I laugh at them as often as I can.'

– Pride and Prejudice

'I call it a very fine country – the hills are steep, the woods seem full of fine timber, and the valley looks comfortable and snug – with rich meadows and several neat farm houses scattered here and there. It exactly answers my idea of a fine country, because it unites beauty with utility – and I dare say it is a picturesque one too, because you admire it...'

– Sense and Sensibility

A View from Richmond Hill looking west towards Twickenham. Drawn and engraved by Richard Havell, 1814 Image taken from *A Series of Picturesque Views of Noblemen's & Gentlemen's seats: with historical and descriptive Accounts.* Engraved in aquatinta by R. Havell & Son (after designs by William Havell and others), London, 1823. [199.i.4, plate 1]

September

1

2

3

4

5

6

7

8

'One half of the world cannot understand
the pleasures of the other.'

– Emma

September

9

10

11

12

September

13

14

15

16

17

18

19

20

'We had a beautiful walk home by Moonlinght.'

– Letter to Cassandra, 8 September 1816

September

21

22

23

24

MARY CRAWFORD DISCUSSES
THE CONVEYANCE OF HER HARP
WITH EDMUND BERTRAM:

—

'Not by a wagon or cart; Oh! No, nothing
of that kind could be hired in the village...
Guess my surprise, when I found that I had been
asking the most unreasonable, most impossible
thing in the world, had offended all the farmers,
all the labourers, all the hay in the parish.'

– *Mansfield Park, Volume I, Chapter 6*

September

25

26

27

28

29

30

'Another world must be unfurled,
Another language known.'

– Verses for Anna

'...you look across the bowling green, behind the house, to a beautiful hanging wood, and on the other side you have a view of the church and village, and beyond them, of those fine bold hills that we have so often admired.'

– *Pride and Prejudice*

View of Godmersham Park, Kent from *Illustrations of Kent, Vol. XI*, 18th–19th centuries. Godmersham Park was the home of Jane Austen's brother Edward and Jane visited there with her sister. [Add. 32363, ff.103v–104]

October

1

2

3

4

5

6

1767 Jane Austen's brother Edward Austen is born

7

8

'This is a charming day.'

– Sanditon

October

9

10

11

12

'Hyde Park. Tom and his Cousin, dashing among Pinks in Rotten Row' taken from *Real life in London*, illustrated by H. Alken and W. Read, London, 1822. [1509/4069 volume I, opposite 24]

October

13

14

15

16

17

18

19

20

'...a curiosity so justly awakened...'

– *Northanger Abbey*

October

21

22

23

24   1798 Jane Austen's writing desk is rescued by Mr Notley

OH WHAT A FINE FELLOW...

—

'He was a piece of Perfection,
noisy Perfection himself, which
I always recollect with regard.'

– *Letter to Francis Austen,
3 July 1813, Chawton*

October

25

26

27

28

29

1811 *Sense & Sensibility* published, advertised as 'a new novel by a Lady'

30

31

'We were in a mood for contemplation...'

– *Love and Friendship, Letter the 13th*

'I had the pleasure of receiving, unpacking & approving our Wedgwood ware... a good match, tho' I think they might have allowed us rather larger leaves, especially in such a Year of fine foliage as this.'

– Letter to Cassandra
6 June 1811, Chawton

Wedgwood and Byerley, York Street, St. James's Square, London Originally published in *Ackermann*, 1809. [Maps.K.Top.27.24]

November

1

1797 Revd. George Austen offers *First Impressions* to the publisher Mr Cadell who rejects it by return of post, sight unseen.

2

3

4

5

6

7

8

'Fine dancing, I believe, like virtue, must be its own reward.'

– *Emma*

November

9

10

11

12

November

13

1815 Jane Austen visits Carlton House to see the Prince Regent's Library

14

15

16

1798 Jane Austen's nephew James Edward Austen is born

17

18

19

20

'Why not seize the pleasure at once, how often is happiness
destroyed by preparation, foolish preparations.'

– *Emma*

November

21

22

23

24

...THE GREATEST BLESSING OF ALL...

—

'Know your own happiness.'

– Sense and Sensibility

November

25

26

1791 Jane Austen finishes *The History of England*

27

28

29

30

'But it is not in my power to delay my journey for one day!'

– Sense and Sensibility

'Henry & I went to the
Exhibition in Spring Gardens...
I was very well pleased—particularly
with a small portrait of Mrs.
Bingley, excessively like her. I
went in hopes of seeing one of
her Sister, but there was no Mrs.
Darcy. — Mrs. Bingley's is exactly
herself, size, shaped face, features
& sweetness; there was never a
greater likeness. She is dressed
in a white gown, with green
ornaments, which convinces
me what I had always supposed,
that green was a favourite colour
with her.'

– Letter to Cassandra Austen
24 May 1813, Sloane Street, London.

'A shilling well laid out. Tom and Jerry at the
Exhibition of Pictures at the Royal Academy' taken
from *Tom and Jerry Life in London, etc.* Edited by J. C.
Hotten with illustrations by I. R. and G. Cruikshank,
London, 1823. [838.i.2, opposite 341]

December

1

2

3

4

December

5

6

7

8

'I had a letter the other day.'

– The Watsons

December

9

10

11

12

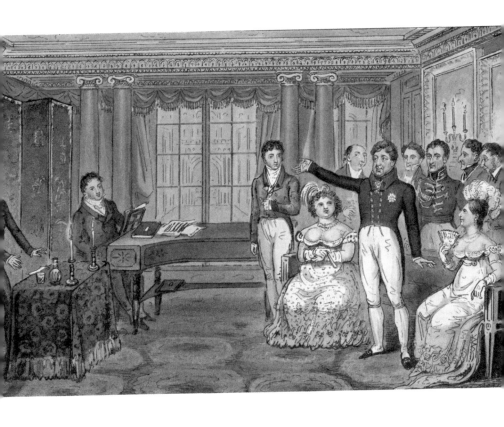

December

13

14

15

16   1775 Jane Austen is born at Steventon in Hampshire

17

18

1817 *Persuasion* and *Northanger Abbey* published

19

20

'The day was uncommonly lovely.'

– *Mansfield Park*

December

21

22

23   1815 *Emma* published

24

REJOICING, DEEP AND SILENT...

—

'I wish you joy.'

– Pride and Prejudice

December

25

26

27

1808 Jane Austen writes to Cassandra, 'I consider everybody as having a right to marry once in their Lives for Love if they can.'

28

29

30

31

'I must learn to be content with being happier than I deserve.'

– Pride and Prejudice

'It was, indeed, a triumphant day...'

– *Mansfield Park*

'I do not write for such dull elves
As have not a great deal of ingenuity themselves.'

– Letter to Cassandra, Friday, 29 January 1813, Chawton

'I liked my solitary elegance very much, and was ready
to laugh all the time at my being where I was.'

– Letter to Cassandra, 24 May 1813, London

And how convinced,
It will all other Hou
That ever have been
With rooms concise,
You'll find us very
Perhaps with Cha
For now it often do
To fancy them fine